Tornado

by Stephen Kramer

NATURE IN ACTION

Lerner Publications / Minneapolis

This book is available in two editions:
Library binding by Lerner Publications Company,
 a division of Lerner Publishing Group, Inc.
Soft cover by First Avenue Editions,
 an imprint of Lerner Publishing Group, Inc.
241 First Avenue North
Minneapolis, MN 55401 USA

For reading levels and more information,
look up this title at www.lernerbooks.com.

Acknowledgements:
Front cover photograph by E. R. Degginger. Back cover courtesy of Indiana Farm Bureau. National Weather Service, Minneapolis: pp. 1, 5, 8, 31, 36; National Center for Atmospheric Research/National Science Foundation: 2 (Richard Filhart), 9, 14, 15, and 17 (Eugene W. McCaul), 35 (Thomas Bettge), 39 40, 41; © Mogil: 4, 27; Weatherstock: 6, 24, and 26-27 (© Keith Brewster), 7 (© Edi Ann Otto), 25 (© Roy Britt), 10, 18 23 right, 44, and 46 top (© Warren Faidley), 19, 20 (NOAA), 21 and 43 (© W. Balzer), 46 bottom (© M. H. Black); Environmental Science Services Administration: 11; © David Manguarian: 12 left; © Jerg Kroener: 12 right; Minnesota Department of Natural Resources: 22, 23 left; State Historical Society of Missouri: 28; Illinois State Historical Library: 29 top; U. of Southern Indiana Special Collections/University Archives: 29 bottom; © Judith Liason: 30; Greene County Historical Society: 34; National Severe Storms Laboratory, National Oceanic and Atmospheric Association (NOAA): 38.
 Illustration on p. 47 by Darren Erickson. Maps based on the studies of Dr. T. Theodore Fujita and the materials produced by the NOAA. Will Keller's quotation originally appeared in the Monthly Weather Review (May 1930), published by the U.S. Weather Bureau.

METRIC CONVERSION CHART		
To find measurements that are almost equal		
WHEN YOU KNOW:	MULTIPLY BY:	TO FIND:
feet	30.48	centimeters
yards	0.91	meters
miles	1.61	kilometers

Library of Congress Cataloging-in-Publication Data

Kramer, Stephen P.
 Tornado / by Stephen Kramer.
  p. cm. — (Nature in action)
 Summary: Describes the formation, different types, and study of tornadoes.
  ISBN-13: 978–0–87614–660–6 (lib. bdg. : alk. paper)
  ISBN-10: 0–87614–660–4 (lib. bdg. : alk. paper)
  ISBN-13: 978–1–57505–058–4 (pbk. : alk. paper)
  ISBN-10: 1–57505–058–7 (pbk. : alk. paper)
  1. Tornadoes—Juvenile literature. [1. Tornadoes.] I. Title.
 II. Series: Nature in action (Minneapolis, Minn.)
QC955.K73 1992
551.55'3—dc20   92-42520

Manufactured in the United States of America
13 – BP – 12/1/15

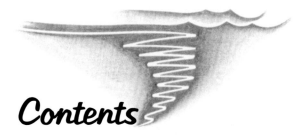

Contents

*For Grandpa Bill and
Grandma Martha*

With thanks to Frederick Ostby, Director of the National Severe Storms Forecast Center, Kansas City, Missouri, and Pat Timm, Northwest Weather Specialist, for their assistance with this book.

On a warm spring afternoon, the air is clear and the sun is bright. Puffy white clouds gather in the sky. It's beginning to seem like summer.

Then some of the clouds start to grow.

They gather into one big storm cloud that billows high into the air. The bottom of the cloud flattens out and reaches across the sky. Winds blow and whirl.

6

Suddenly, a funnel of twisting winds drops out of the storm cloud and swoops toward the earth. The swirling storm touches down, kicking up dust and dirt. The winds roar and howl like a dozen screaming jet planes. A tornado races across the countryside.

The tornado rips houses off their foundations. It picks up cars and trucks, and throws them around as if they were toys. Trees are uprooted and scattered about.

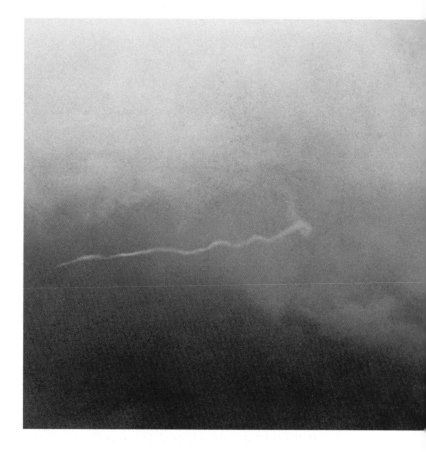

Then, as it swirls through an open field, the tornado begins to change. It becomes long and thin, like a piece of rope. The tornado stretches sideways through the air.

A few minutes later, the tornado is gone—vanished as quickly and mysteriously as it appeared.

What Is a Tornado?

A tornado is a powerful, twisting windstorm. It begins high in the air, among the winds of a giant storm cloud. People who have watched a tornado's howling winds reach down from the sky have said it's the most frightening thing they have ever seen. In some parts of the United States, these windstorms are called twisters or cyclones.

Tornadoes are not the only whirling windstorms that move through the earth's air. Dust devils, hurricanes, and typhoons all have twisting winds. But these windstorms differ from tornadoes in important ways.

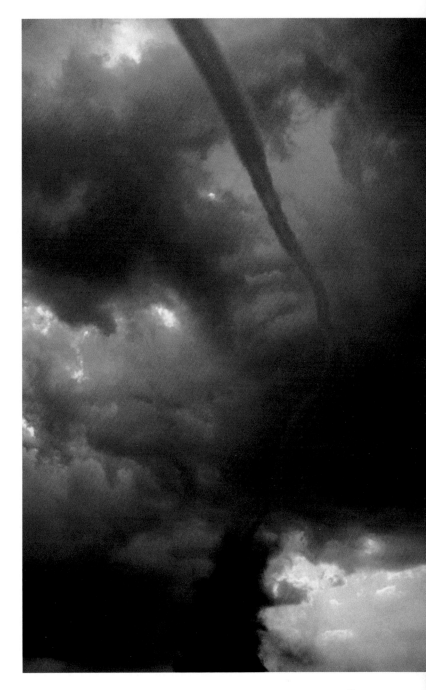

Dust devils are the weakest of the swirling windstorms. Their winds usually spin between 12 and 30 miles per hour. Most dust devils are less than five feet across, and few last more than a minute or two. They are often seen in desert areas under clear skies. Dust devils form near the ground when certain kinds of winds make hot, rising air start to spin.

Hurricanes and typhoons are the largest of the swirling windstorms. The winds of these storms blow about 75 to 150 miles per hour. They form over warm, tropical oceans and cause heavy rains as well as strong winds. When a tropical storm like this begins over the Atlantic Ocean or the eastern Pacific Ocean, it is called a hurricane. The same kind of storm in the western Pacific Ocean or the Indian Ocean is called a typhoon. Hurricanes and typhoons may be several hundred miles wide, travel thousands of miles, and last for days.

Tornadoes are not as large as hurricanes and typhoons, and they don't travel as far. In fact, many tornadoes last only a few minutes. But the spinning winds of a tornado can rip through the air at up to 300 miles per hour. The winds of a large tornado are the fastest, most dangerous winds on earth.

How Do Tornadoes Form?

On a beautiful spring day, the sun is shining across the southern United States. Warm, moist air swirls out of the Gulf of Mexico. It drifts to the north, heating the land and reminding people that summer is not far away.

Far to the north, the nights are still long. Cool, dry air from the central part of Canada spills downward into the United States. The cool air is guided south and east by the Rocky Mountains. It carries biting winds and a reminder that winter has just ended.

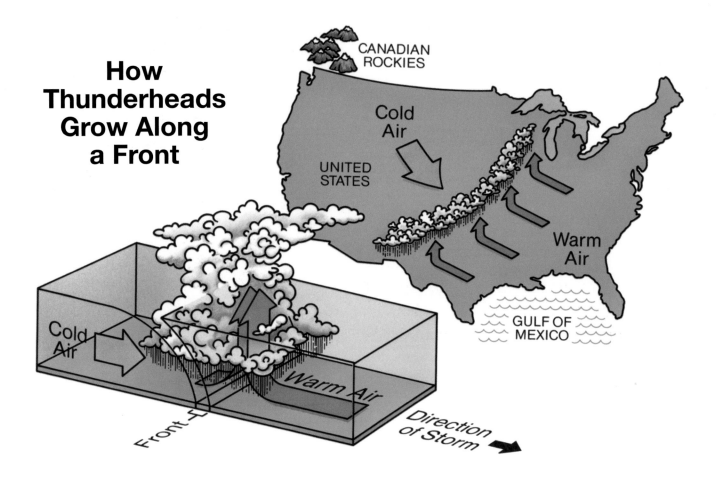

How Thunderheads Grow Along a Front

CANADIAN ROCKIES

Cold Air

UNITED STATES

Warm Air

GULF OF MEXICO

Cold Air

Warm Air

Front

Direction of Storm

Fronts

In the middle of the United States, the cool air pushes against the warm air. The place where the two kinds of air meet is called a front. A front can stretch over a hundred miles.

As the cool air presses forward, it slides underneath the warm air. The warm air is pushed upward, and water droplets form. Fast-growing clouds take shape. These clouds are called thunderheads. A line of thunderheads a hundred or more miles long may grow along a front.

13

Thunderheads

Thunderheads, or cumulonimbus (kyu-mya-lo-NIM-buhs) clouds, are the giant clouds that produce storms with lightning and thunder. When you see a thunderhead, you are looking at a place in the sky where warm, moist air is rising quickly through cool air. This can happen along and ahead of fronts as well as just on hot, sunny days.

When the sun heats up the ground, the air near it grows warm too. The warm air rises, but sometimes it gets trapped by a layer of cooler air above it. As the day goes on, the sun keeps shining, and more heated air pushes its way skyward. Finally, it breaks through. The warm air blasts high into the sky, like water shooting up from a fountain, and a thunderhead grows.

The thunderheads most likely to cause tornadoes are the ones that form along and ahead of fronts. This is because strong winds often blow high above fronts. The power of these winds, along with slower winds closer to the ground, can make the rising air in a thunderhead start spinning.

As the winds in a thunderhead swirl, the bottom of the cloud stretches out across the sky and the top of the cloud towers upward. The mesocyclone is forming to the far right of these photographs.

Mesocyclones

If the rising air in a thunderhead begins to spin, the column of spinning winds is called a mesocyclone (mez-uh-SY-klon). As a mesocyclone twirls, it stretches toward warm air near the ground. The lower part of the mesocyclone narrows. The narrower it becomes, the faster it spins—just as figure skaters and dancers twirl faster when they pull their arms close to their bodies.

The mesocyclone acts like a giant vacuum-cleaner hose. Warm air is sucked up through the lower end of the mesocyclone and pulled upward through the thunderhead. The air swirls higher and higher. The spinning air may soar all the way to the top of a thunderhead, 10 miles above the ground.

Some mesocyclones spin like this for a few minutes and then just disappear. In others, however, a smaller column of faster-spinning air forms inside the bottom of the mesocyclone. This column is usually less than a half mile wide. As it spins, it reaches toward the ground.

How a Funnel Cloud Forms

When the cold air slides under the warm air and pushes it upward, a thunderhead can develop. The rising winds often start to spin. If the winds twirl fast enough, a mesocyclone may form. As the warm, wet air soars, it cools, and rain falls. Once the air rises above the freezing line (where the temperature is lower than 32°F), the water droplets in the air turn to hail. The winds may increase in speed, and a funnel cloud can form at the base of the mesocyclone.

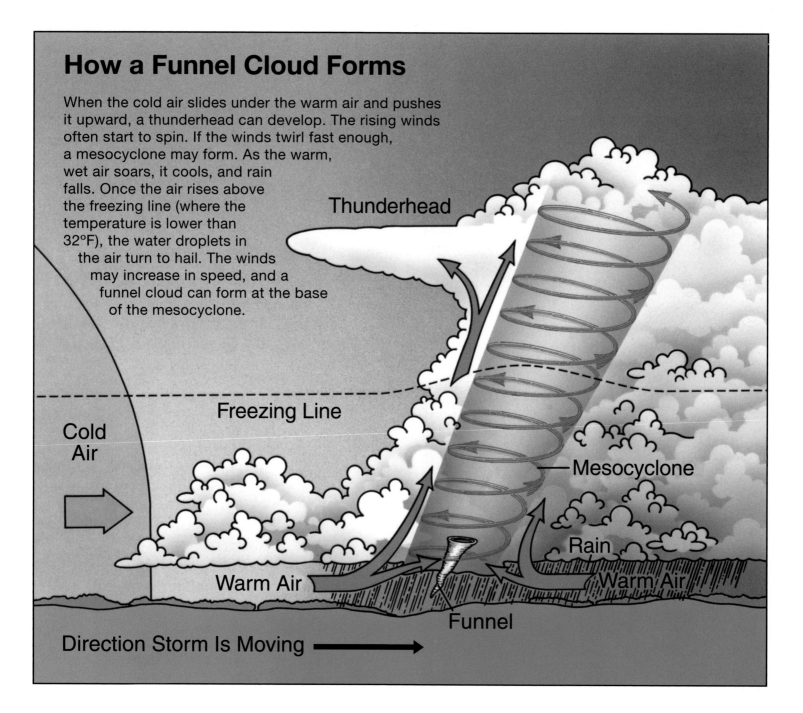

Thunderhead

Freezing Line

Cold Air

Mesocyclone

Warm Air

Rain

Warm Air

Funnel

Direction Storm Is Moving

Funnel Clouds

When the column of tightly spinning winds dips down from the mesocyclone, it sucks up warm, moist air. The air cools as it is pulled up into the column. Tiny droplets of water form, and a whirling cloud appears. This cloud is called a funnel cloud.

Funnel clouds are named for their shape. They are often shaped like funnels—tubes that are wide at the top and narrow at the bottom. Some funnel clouds hang straight down from the storm cloud. Others stretch sideways through the sky. A funnel cloud may dip down and then lift back up into the mesocyclone. Or it may touch ground. If it does, the funnel cloud is called a tornado.

Sometimes when a tornado is forming, no funnel cloud can be seen. The air near the ground is so dry that when it is sucked into the whirling column, no water droplets form. Then the fast-spinning air stays invisible until it becomes a tornado—stirring up dust and soil.

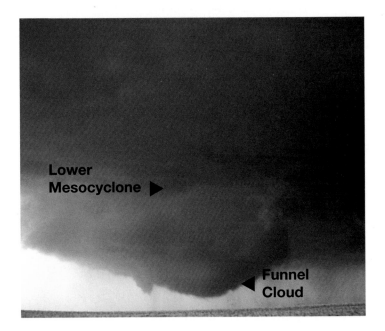

Lower Mesocyclone ▶

◀ Funnel Cloud

◀ Tornado

Tornadoes

The winds of a large tornado can cut like a saw through forests, farms, and cities. Sticks, rocks, and broken glass become as dangerous as bullets. A tornado can twist railroad tracks into candy-cane shapes or pluck all the feathers off of a chicken. It can blast pieces of wood through a wall as if they had been shot from a cannon.

If you see a funnel cloud dip down from a thunderhead, it's usually a sign that a tornado is on its way. But not all tornadoes look like funnels. They can be shaped more like jars—with the same width from top to bottom. Or they may have more than one funnel. Large tornadoes may have several narrow, twisting funnels circling around like horses on a merry-go-round.

Some of the largest, most dangerous tornadoes don't look like funnels at all. These tornadoes appear to be big clouds moving along the ground. People often think they are rainstorms or smoke from fires.

Tornadoes also change shape over time. Many funnels become thin, like pieces of rope, as they lose power. They look like giant elephant trunks snaking through the sky.

19

As tornadoes travel across the land, they pick up dust, soil, and whatever else is on the ground. These things give a tornado its color. Many people think of tornadoes as gray or black. But a tornado moving across a field of red soil in Georgia or Oklahoma will become a reddish color. A tornado roaring over a freshly plowed brown field in Texas will become brown. And a few white tornadoes may even be seen, swirling across fields of snow.

A tornado also looks different to people seeing it from different places. If you see a tornado with rain falling behind it, the tornado will probably appear light in color. However, if you could see the same tornado from the opposite side, with the sun and a light sky behind it, the funnel would appear darker.

Although tornadoes can cause great destruction, they are an important part of the Earth's weather patterns. A tornado, like the whistle on a teakettle, helps let off pressure that builds up in the atmosphere. In addition, the storms that produce tornadoes often bring much needed rain.

Tornado Paths

When powerful tornadoes move along the ground, they leave behind trails of destruction. Telephone poles are snapped off at the ground. Automobiles look as if they have been run over by an enormous lawnmower. And where a house once stood, there is only a pile of splintered boards, broken glass, and twisted pipes. These trails of destruction are called tornado paths or tracks.

Because the winds of a tornado swirl in such a tight funnel, a tornado path is not much wider than the bottom of the tornado. Objects only a few feet on each side of a tornado's path may not be harmed at all. Tornadoes have been known to peel walls off buildings and leave the furniture inside undisturbed.

The length of a tornado path depends on how fast a tornado is moving and how much time it spends on the ground. Some tornadoes touch down and move across the land until they lose their power. Others travel along the ground for a while, lift into the sky, and then touch down again elsewhere. They skip across the countryside as if they were playing hopscotch.

A tornado stripped these trees of their branches and leaves, but left them standing.

After a tornado has passed, its path can usually be seen clearly from an airplane. Sometimes tornadoes leave paths as straight as bowling lanes. Other times, they travel in curved, looping trails. These tornadoes leave winding paths of damage.

23

Kinds of Tornadoes

When people hear the word tornado, they usually think of a huge windstorm that destroys everything in its path. But most tornadoes are not this powerful. To help describe differences in the strength of tornadoes, scientists divide them into three categories: weak, strong, and violent.

Weak Tornadoes

If a tornado's winds spin at 112 miles per hour or less, scientists consider the tornado weak. Winds of 112 miles per hour are very fast—about twice as fast as cars speeding along highways. But these winds are still slow when compared to the winds in other tornadoes.

Weak tornadoes usually leave behind a path of damage less than 3 miles long. The path is usually less than 50 yards wide.

Weak tornadoes are the most common of the three tornado types. About 800 tornadoes are reported in the United States each year, and over ¾ of them are weak. Although the winds of these tornadoes are dangerous, few people are killed by them.

Strong Tornadoes

Strong tornadoes have winds ranging from 113 to 206 miles per hour. These tornadoes cut a path about 9 miles long and 200 yards wide. Fewer than ¼ of the tornadoes reported in the United States each year are strong. Yet, because of their faster winds and longer paths, strong tornadoes are often killers.

Violent Tornadoes

Violent tornadoes are the least common type of tornado. Only about 1 in 50 tornadoes in the United States is classified as violent. These tornadoes may have winds ranging from 207 to about 300 miles per hour. They may last several hours. A typical violent tornado leaves a path of destruction about 26 miles long and 425 yards wide. A few violent tornadoes have left paths over 100 miles long and 1 mile wide.

A violent tornado can pick up buildings and set them down in other places—just as the tornado did in the *The Wizard of Oz*. A Kansas tornado once picked up a whole herd of steers. A person who was watching said that the cows sailed through the air like a flock of birds. In 1958, another Kansas tornado pulled a woman out of her house through a window and set her down, alive, 60 feet away—right next to a broken phonograph record called "Stormy Weather."

Although tornadoes sometimes carry people through the air without harming them, most people who are picked up by a violent tornado do not live to tell about it. About ¾ of the people who die in the United States each year because of tornadoes are killed by these powerful storms.

Tri-State Tornado March 18, 1925

ILLINOIS

INDIANA

MISSOURI

Mississippi R.

2:26 pm
2:34 pm
2:38 pm

4:00 pm
4:18 pm
4:30 pm
END

2:00 pm
1:15 pm

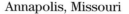

7 8
9 11
10

3 4 5 6

1 2

1:01 pm
1

The tornado traveled 219 miles on the ground.

1 (north of) Ellington
2 Annapolis
3 Biehle
4 Gorham
5 Murphysboro
6 De Soto

7 West Frankfort
8 Parrish
9 Griffin
10 Owensville
11 Princeton

The United States is well known for the fury of its twisters. The greatest number of violent tornadoes and the most destructive ones on earth happen on the American plains.

The deadliest tornado in United States history struck on March 18, 1925. It has been named the Tri-State tornado because it roared through three states. The Tri-State Tornado is believed to be the largest single tornado ever to hit the United States.

The tornado touched down just outside of Annapolis, Missouri, shortly after one o'clock in the afternoon. Its funnel was a gray-white color, because the swirling winds hadn't yet picked up much dust and soil. The tornado headed right for the middle of Annapolis. It roared down Main Street, destroying nearly every building on the street.

28

Annapolis, Missouri

From the southeast corner of Missouri, the tornado swept east into Illinois and then into Indiana. For three and a half hours, it tore through farmlands and small towns. According to some witnesses, the sound it made was "like a thousand freight trains."

De Soto, a small town in Illinois, was completely demolished. After the tornado ripped through, there wasn't a building taller than 10 feet high left standing. Of De Soto's 600 residents, 118 died and 200 were injured.

By the time it finally disappeared, the Tri-State Tornado had left behind a path of destruction 219 miles long. Towns were destroyed, trees ripped out of the ground, and entire families killed or injured. In a single afternoon, the tornado killed 689 people, injured 2,000, and left 11,000 people homeless.

De Soto, Illinois

Griffin, Indiana

Waterspouts

Besides weak, strong, and violent tornadoes, there are also waterspouts. Waterspouts are very much like tornadoes, but they move over water instead of land. Some waterspouts form when a funnel cloud dips down from a thunderhead and touches a lake, river, or ocean. Others form when a tornado moves from land to water.

Another kind of waterspout forms just above the water on sunny days when there are no thunderheads in the area. These twisters are called fair-weather waterspouts.

Most waterspouts last only a few minutes. They usually are smaller than tornadoes and have slower winds. But waterspouts can be dangerous. The winds of a large waterspout can sink a small boat.

If a waterspout moves onto land, it becomes a tornado. Some tornadoes that were once ocean waterspouts carry salty spray with them. These tornadoes may travel miles inland and then send down showers of salty rain.

Waterspouts are often seen over the warm waters of the Atlantic and Indian Oceans, the Mediterranean Sea, and the Gulf of Mexico. During the summer, the southern coast of Florida is a good place to look for them. Waterspouts also appear over lakes in the central part of the United States—especially during the spring and summer.

Where and When Do Tornadoes Happen?

Scientists think that over 1,000 tornadoes happen throughout the world every year. Because North America is so widely known for its large, violent tornadoes, many people think of tornadoes as windstorms that happen only in the United States and Canada. Tornadoes, however, dip down from the clouds in many other parts of the world—including places such as Australia, Japan, New Zealand, India, and parts of Africa and South America. Also, in warm places surrounded by water, such as Italy and islands in the Pacific Ocean, ocean waterspouts often turn into tornadoes.

It's not easy to make an accurate count of how many tornadoes happen each year. Weak tornadoes are not always seen or reported. And when tornadoes occur in areas where people live or where there is no government agency keeping track, they are rarely recorded.

Areas with the Greatest Tornado Danger

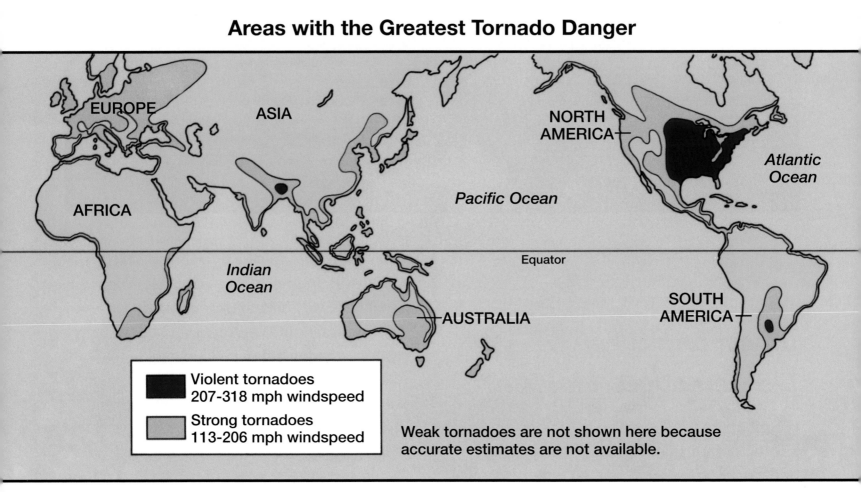

EUROPE

ASIA

NORTH AMERICA

Atlantic Ocean

AFRICA

Pacific Ocean

Indian Ocean

Equator

AUSTRALIA

SOUTH AMERICA

Violent tornadoes
207-318 mph windspeed

Strong tornadoes
113-206 mph windspeed

Weak tornadoes are not shown here because accurate estimates are not available.

Average Number of Tornadoes per 10-Year Period

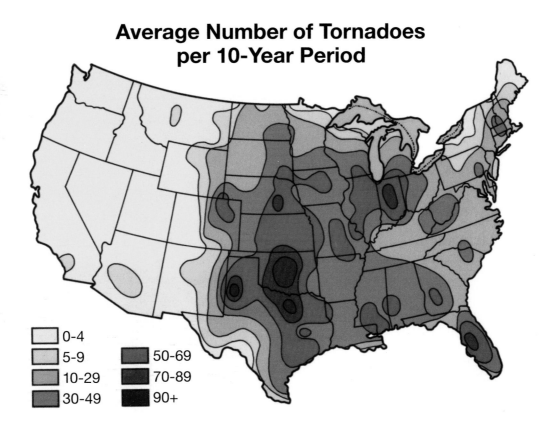

0-4
5-9
10-29
30-49
50-69
70-89
90+

In the United States, tornadoes have been reported in each of the 50 states, but they are most common in the south-central part of the nation. So many tornadoes travel through a strip of land in Missouri, Kansas, Oklahoma, and northern Texas that the area has been nicknamed "Tornado Alley."

People living in North America are most likely to see tornadoes in the spring and summer. This is when cool air rushing southeast from the Arctic and the Canadian Rockies meets warm air sweeping north from the Gulf of Mexico, and enormous fronts form. Overhead, a strong wind called the jet stream blows from the west. This wind helps make the thunderheads that grow along the fronts start spinning. In a single afternoon, dozens of tornadoes may drop down from these thunderheads.

In the spring of 1974, the largest outbreak of tornadoes ever recorded swept across the central part of the United States. During the afternoon of April 3 and the early morning hours of April 4, *148* tornadoes churned through 13 states. Towns such as Xenia, Ohio, and Brandenburg, Kentucky, were nearly demolished. The tornadoes killed 315 people, injured more than 6,000 others, and destroyed over 9,600 homes.

Scenes from Xenia, Ohio, after the 1974 Tornado Outbreak

Models of the world on a weather-station computer screen.

Tornadoes dip down from thunderheads at different times of the year in different countries. In Germany and France, tornadoes are most common in the middle or toward the end of summer. The middle of winter is tornado season on the west coast of Japan. In Australia and New Zealand, tornadoes happen all year long.

35

Studying Tornadoes

Very few people anywhere in the world have ever seen the inside of a tornado. One stormy day, however, a Kansas farmer named Will Keller looked up into a tornado that passed right over his head. It happened in 1928, as he was hurrying his family to their cellar. A hailstorm had just destroyed the Kellers' wheat field, and a tornado was headed directly for them. As Will was closing the door to the cellar, he looked back at the tornado. It was beginning to lift off the ground. Instead of going into the cellar, Will waited and watched:

At last the great shaggy end of the funnel hung directly overhead. Everything was as still as death. There was a strong gassy odor and it seemed that I could not breathe.

There was a screaming, hissing sound coming directly from the end of the funnel. I looked up and to my astonishment I saw right up into the heart of the tornado. There was a circular opening ... about 50 or 100 feet in diameter, and extending straight upward for a distance of at least one-half mile ... The walls of this opening were of rotating clouds and the whole was made brilliantly visible by constant flashes of lightning which zigzagged from side to side. Had it not been for the lightning, I could not have seen the opening. . . . Around the lower rim of the great [funnel,] small tornadoes were constantly forming and breaking away. These looked like tails as they writhed their way around the end of the funnel. It was these that made the hissing noise.

Not many people who get such a close view of a tornado survive its deadly winds, so scientists pay attention to stories like the one by Will Keller. Reports of how tornadoes look, sound, and behave helped scientists learn more about these storms. Studying tornado paths and the damage tornadoes leave can also provide clues. But neither stories nor damage can tell the whole story about what really happens inside the swirling funnels.

Every spring, scientists spend days driving around the back roads of Texas and Oklahoma, trying to get close enough to tornadoes to observe them. One of their goals is to place scientific instruments in the tornadoes' paths. This is difficult and dangerous work.

Most tornadoes in the United States move from the southwest toward the northeast. But even so, trying to predict where a tornado will head is almost impossible. Tornadoes form, race along the ground, and disappear—often within a matter of a few minutes. They can move over the ground at 70 miles or more per hour. They may hover in one spot for a short time or turn around and head back in the direction from which they came. For these reasons, anyone near a tornado is in danger. That is why trying to see a tornado up close should be left to experts.

Fortunately, there are ways to study tornadoes in laboratories. Some scientists have developed special rooms where they can create swirling winds and watch small tornadoes form. Scientists can also use computers to make models showing the speed and direction of winds in thunderheads or mesocyclones. By learning more about these winds, scientists can make better predictions about which storms will cause tornadoes.

Doppler radar

Doppler radar room

Predicting Tornadoes

Every year, the United States has between 50,000 and 100,000 thunderstorms. But only about 1 out of 100 of these thunderstorms creates a tornado.

One of the best tools for studying tornado-causing thunderstorms is Doppler radar. Doppler radar can measure the speeds and directions of the winds in thunderstorms. This information helps scientists know whether or not a mesocyclone is forming inside a storm.

Experts at the National Severe Storms Forecast Center, in Kansas City, Missouri, keep a constant watch on weather patterns across the United States. They collect information from Doppler radar, other radar, local weather stations, satellite photographs, and airline pilot reports. By charting temperatures, wind speeds, and the amounts of moisture in the air, scientists can pinpoint the storms most likely to cause tornadoes.

The Mile High Radar station, northeast of Denver, Colorado, is one of the first NEXRAD (Next Generation Weather Radar) stations completed. Scientists would like a network of these Doppler radar stations built across the United States.

During the early morning hours, the Forecast Center makes predictions about areas in the United States where strong thunderstorms are expected to develop later in the day. Local weather offices use these predictions to prepare their daily weather forecasts.

When fronts move into an area and strong thunderstorms are forming, the Forecast Center sends out a notice called a *Tornado Watch*. A Tornado Watch means that weather that might produce tornadoes is in the area. Local radio and television stations announce the watch, letting people know they should be prepared for a tornado. A watch usually lasts about six hours.

If a tornado has actually been seen or detected by radar, the local Weather Service Office issues a *Tornado Warning*. A Tornado Warning means that people should get to a safe place immediately because a tornado is nearby. Television and radio stations broadcast the warning, telling where the tornado has been seen and where it is headed. In many communities, sirens are also used to alert people that a tornado is nearby.

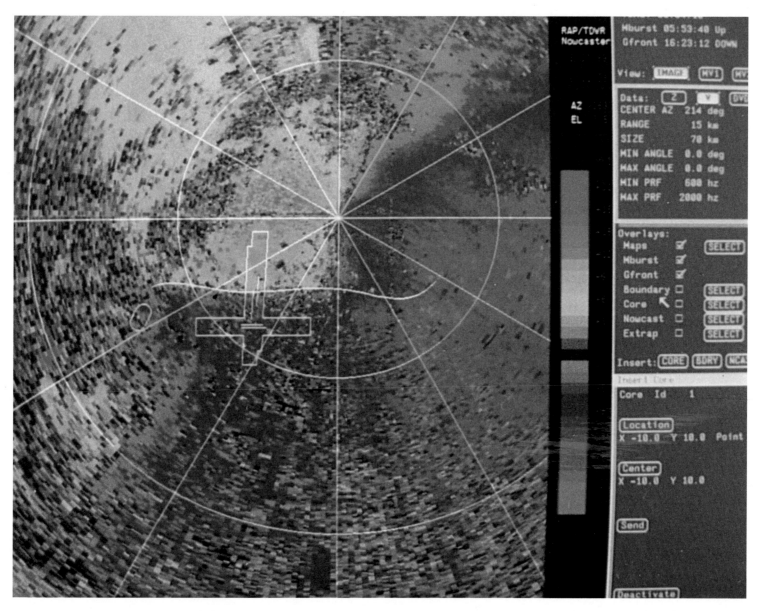

This picture is from an advanced weather workstation. The colors show moving air detected by Doppler radar. The yellow and orange areas show winds blowing in one direction (from the top left of the screen to the bottom right). The white line across the picture shows a dividing line where the winds shift. Underneath this line, the winds are blowing in the opposite direction (bottom right to top left). Showers may form where the winds meet (along the white line).

Safety Tips

Because most tornadoes are small and last a short time, you'll probably never find yourself in a tornado's path. Even in Tornado Alley, the chances of being caught in a tornado are not very high. On average, a building in Tornado Alley will be struck by a tornado only once every 250 years. Still, if a tornado should ever suddenly appear in your area, knowing tornado safety rules may be a life-or-death matter. In the United States, about 80 people are killed by tornadoes every year.

Before tornado season arrives, talk to your parents about setting up a tornado shelter. A shelter is a safe place for you to stay when a tornado is near. The safest place to have a shelter is in a basement. Pick a spot in your basement that is away from any windows. Do not choose a place where there is a heavy object, such as a piano or refrigerator, on the floor above you.

Store food, water, blankets, a flashlight, something to do to pass the time (such as a game or book) and a battery-powered radio in your shelter.

Many apartment buildings already have a place set aside for a tornado shelter. If you live in an apartment without a shelter, ask the manager where you should go. If you live in a mobile home, make plans to go to a building where you will be safe. Your shelter may be a neighbor's basement or a nearby public building. Do not stay in a mobile home or automobile if a tornado is in the area. Tornadoes often send mobile homes and cars sailing through the air, twisting them out of shape and blasting them full of broken glass and pieces of metal.

If your house or apartment doesn't have a basement, you can take shelter in a hallway, closet, or small room toward the inside of the building. Stay away from windows. Tornado winds often shatter them, sending bits of glass flying.

If you live in an area where tornadoes occur, pay attention to weather reports on the radio and television—especially during tornado season.

If a Tornado Watch is announced, keep listening and follow directions. If the news announcer tells you the watch has been changed to a warning, or if you hear sirens or strong winds, go to your shelter immediately. If you are in a store, mall, or other public building, stay calm and listen for instructions. Someone will tell you about a safe place to go. If you are outside and cannot get to a building in time, hurry to the lowest nearby spot—a ravine, a ditch by the roadside, or a drain pipe beneath the road. Lie down and cover your head with your hands.

In areas where tornadoes happen frequently, schools have tornado drills. Students learn where to go and what to do for safety if a tornado is near. If you are at school when a tornado approaches, stay calm and follow your teacher's instructions.

Since lightning often flashes around tornadoes, also obey lightning safety rules. Stay away from metal objects. Use the telephone only for emergencies. Most important, remember that if a Tornado Watch is changed to a Tornado Warning, go to a safe place immediately. Don't risk your life by staying outside to watch a tornado!

People who have seen a tornado's power have learned to keep a watch on the sky. Tornadoes will dip down out of the clouds whenever weather conditions are right. Their amazing funnels will leave trails of destruction through farmlands, small towns and large cities. Nothing we can do will turn a tornado in a different direction, make it a single minute shorter, or lessen its power.

A tornado is a spectacular reminder of the power of the earth's winds.

45

Fascinating Facts

The word tornado comes from the Spanish word tronado, which means "thunderstorm." In Japan, tornadoes are called tatsumaki, which means "dragon whirls."

Sailors used to believe they could destroy a waterspout with a well-aimed cannon shot.

In the northern half of the world, the winds of a tornado usually swirl counter-clockwise. This means that if you could watch the tornado from above, you would see its winds spin the opposite direction the hands of a clock turn. In the southern half of the world, the winds usually spin clockwise—the same direction the hands of a clock turn.

A tornado once picked up an engine from the Union Pacific Railroad, turned it around, and set it back down on a parallel track facing the opposite direction.

46

A tornado embedded a fork in this tree in Saragosa, Texas.

Some scientists believe that a small tornado touched down in this wheatfield in East Devon, England, making this "magic circle."

You will probably never see it rain cats and dogs, but one day you could see it rain frogs or fish. Scientists believe that at times waterspouts pick up large numbers of fish or frogs and then drop them in showers, miles from where they were swept up.

Tornadoes traveling across soils of red clay may pick up red dust and carry it high into the air. When the dust mixes with moisture, it can fall to the earth as red raindrops. At times, people have thought the sky was raining blood.

For many years, people were told to open the windows of their homes before taking shelter. Scientists believed that low air pressure inside a tornado could cause a tightly closed building to explode. Now scientists know that buildings destroyed by tornadoes do not explode—they are ripped apart by the tornados' powerful winds. So stay away from windows and head straight for the basement!

On May 20, 1919, people in Codell, Kansas, were keeping an extra close watch on the sky. Their town had been struck by tornadoes on May 20 of 1916, 1917, and 1918.

In 1931, a tornado in Minnesota picked up an 83-ton railroad coach, carried it 80 feet through the air, and dropped it in a ditch.

Glossary

Cumulonimbus cloud: A tall cloud that can cause thunderstorms and tornadoes. Another name for this cloud is thunderhead.

Cyclone: A name often used for tornadoes, hurricanes, and typhoons

Doppler radar: A kind of radar that helps scientists learn about the speeds and directions of the winds in storms

Dust devil: A small, swirling windstorm often seen in desert areas

Front: The area where two large bodies of air that are different in temperature or moisture meet. When cold air presses forward, the advancing edge is called a cold front. When warm air presses forward, the advancing edge is a warm front. A cold front is more likely to cause tornadoes than a warm front.

Funnel cloud: The swirling winds that dip down from a mesocyclone. If the funnel touches the ground, it becomes a tornado. If it touches down on a lake, ocean, or river, it becomes a waterspout.

Hurricane: A large storm of whirling winds and heavy rain that develops over the Atlantic Ocean or east Pacific Ocean

Mesocyclone: The spinning, rising air of a thunderhead. Under the right conditions, this spinning air can produce a tornado or waterspout.

Thunderhead: A tall cloud that can cause thunderstorms and tornadoes. Another name for thunderhead is cumulonimbus cloud.

Tornado: A powerful, twisting windstorm that begins in the air currents of a thunderhead and reaches down to touch ground

Tornado path: The route of destruction a tornado cuts along the ground as it moves. The path is also called a tornado track.

Tornado shelter: A safe place to stay when a tornado is near

Tornado Warning: A notice, usually broadcast by radio and television stations, that a tornado has been spotted nearby and people should get to a safe place immediately

Tornado Watch: A notice, usually broadcast by radio and television stations, that weather conditions are favorable for producing tornadoes

Twister: Another name for a tornado

Typhoon: A large storm of whirling winds and heavy rains that develops over the west Pacific Ocean or the Indian Ocean

Waterspout: A cloud of whirling winds that moves across water